NATIONAL GEOGRAPHIC

EVERYDAY SCIENCE

Science at the Aquarium

Kate Boehm Jerome

PICTURE CREDITS
Cover background, Owaki-Kulla/Corbis; cover insets (bottom left), Johnny Johnson/Animals Animals, (middle right) Imagesource, Travel Icons/Creatas, (bottom right) Digital Vision, Life Underwater/Creatas, (bottom middle) Digital Vision, Life Underwater/Creatas, (bottom middle) Digital Vision, Life Underwater/Creatas; page 1 (top left), page 4 (top left), page 24 (bottom) Art Explosion; page 1 (middle) The Image Bank/Getty Images; page 3 (bottom middle), page 14 (top left) Photodisc, Sea Life/Creatas; page 4 (bottom left), Richard Cummins/Corbis (New York); page 5 Courtesy of The Newport Aquarium/Newport, KY; page 6 (top left), Gary Conner/Photo Edit; pages 6-7 (bottom), page 19 (top right), Randy Wilder/Monterey Bay Aquarium; page 7 (inset), Dr. Paul A. Zaul/Photo Researchers; page 8 (top left), David Wrobel/Visuals Unlimited; page 9, Sisse Brimberg/National Geographic Image Collection; page 10 (top left), Gerard Lacz/FLPA/Bruce Coleman, Inc.; pages 10-11 (bottom), page 21, page 23 (bottom) The Image Bank/Getty Images; page 11 (inset), page 18 (top left), Philip Colla/Philip Colla Photography; page 12 (top left) Rubberball, Silhouettes of Adults; pages 12-13 (bottom), pages 18-19 (bottom), page 21 (inset), Jonathan Blair/Corbis; page 13 (inset), Jeffrey L. Rotman/Corbis; pages 14-15 (bottom), Denis Tapparel/Under Water Imagery; page 14 (inset), Deb Fugitt/City Seahorse, Inc; page 16 (top left) Image Source, Travel Icons; page 16 (inset), Dave B. Fleetham/Tom Stack & Associates; page 17, Stephen Frink/Corbis; page 18 (bottom left), Bill Curtsinger/National Geographic Image Collection; page 20 (top left) NASA; page 23 (bottom) Robert Pickett/Corbis

Produced through the worldwide resources of the National Geographic Society, John M. Fahey, Jr., President and Chief Executive Officer; Gilbert M. Grosvenor, Chairman of the Board; Nina D. Hoffman, Executive Vice President and President, Books and Education Publishing Group.

PREPARED BY NATIONAL GEOGRAPHIC SCHOOL PUBLISHING
Ericka Markman, Senior Vice President and President, Children's Books and Education Publishing Group; Steve Mico, Vice President, Editorial Director; Rosemary Baker, Executive Editor; Barbara Seeber, Editorial Manager; Jim Hiscott, Design Manager; Kristin Hanneman, Illustrations Manager; Matt Wascavage, Manager of Publishing Services; Sean Philpotts, Production Manager.

MANUFACTURING AND QUALITY MANAGEMENT
Christopher A. Liedel, Chief Financial Officer; Phillip L. Schlosser, Director; Clifton M. Brown, Manager.

PROGRAM DEVELOPMENT
Kate Boehm Jerome

ART DIRECTION
Daniel Banks, Project Design Company

CONSULTANTS/REVIEWERS: Dr. Kathleen Marrs, Assistant Professor of Biology, Indiana University Purdue University Indianapolis; Dr. Randy Kochevar, Marine biologist, Monterey Bay Aquarium

BOOK DEVELOPMENT: The Mazer Corporation

Published by the National Geographic Society
1145 17th Street, N.W.
Washington, D.C. 20036-4688

ISBN: 0-7922-4570-9

Seventh Printing May, 2010
Printed in Canada

Contents

Have you been to an aquarium?

It's like an underwater zoo. Amazing sea creatures are on display—and you don't even have to get wet to see them!

Most people think only about homes, or **habitats,** on land. But many plants and animals live in the water. Did you know there are more than 20,000 different kinds of fish? Aquariums are wonderful places to learn about the underwater creatures we so rarely see.

Visitors at Mandalay Bay Shark Reef in Las Vegas, Nevada

Why don't jellyfish look like fish? How often do whales come up for air? Why do some fish swim in schools? Think of all the interesting questions you can ask about the underwater world.

Speaking of good questions, did you ever wonder . . .

Why are some fish kept in separate exhibits?

Brightly colored fish swim together in one exhibit. Across the hall the exhibit is for seahorses only. Why are they separate?

There are many reasons different fish need different habitats. Some fish need special food. Others need a certain water temperature. Living things in an aquarium survive best in habitats built to meet their needs.

Leafy sea dragon at Monterey Bay Aquarium in Monterey, California

Seahorses, for example, are not strong swimmers. They like sea grasses or weeds in their tank. They use these plants as anchors. They hang on to them with their tails.

Seahorses also like to eat live food. They feed on small shrimp and fish. But they can be slow eaters. In a small aquarium tank, fast-feeding fish can take all the food before the seahorses have a chance to eat. So it's better to keep these beautiful, strange-looking creatures in a special habitat of their own.

Seahorse holding on to a plant

Speaking of looks, did you ever wonder . . .

Why don't jellyfish look like fish?

Purple stripe jellyfish

They look like blobs of see-through jelly. Are these creatures really fish?

As a matter of fact, jellyfish aren't fish. They don't have a backbone. In fact, they have no bones at all. "Jellies" belong to a group of underwater animals called **invertebrates.**

Believe it or not, there are about 200 kinds of jellyfish. Many are tiny, but some are quite large. Since jellyfish have no bones, they are very light. Ocean currents easily carry these creatures in the open seas.

Many jellyfish have **tentacles.** These are long, arm-like structures that dangle from the jelly's main body. Jellies use tentacles as fishing lines. For example, the sea nettle, a type of jellyfish, has stinging cells on its tentacles. When its tentacles touch a tiny fish, the stinging cells paralyze it. The sea nettle then eats the fish.

Jellyfish don't have lungs. They take in oxygen from the water through the outer layers of their bodies. What an interesting way to breathe!

A fleet of golden,
long-tentacled jellyfish

**Speaking of
breathing,
did you ever
wonder . . .**

How often do whales come up for air?

Orca

They swim underwater . . . but they can't stay down too long. Whales need air to breathe.

All whales are **mammals.** This means that they must come to the surface of the water to breathe air. A whale breathes through the blowhole on top of its head.

One type of whale you might see at an aquarium is the beluga whale. A beluga can hold its breath for up to 20 minutes on a dive. Usually, however, a beluga comes up to breathe several times a minute.

The Shedd Aquarium

The Shedd Aquarium in Chicago, Illinois, has a huge tank for beluga whales. The tank holds more than 11 million liters (about 3 million gallons) of salt water. Good thing, too. Although small for whales, the belugas in Chicago are still pretty big. The largest one is about 4 meters (13 feet) long and weighs more than 900 kilograms (about 2,100 pounds).

A humpback whale in Antarctica spouts air from its blowhole.

Beluga whales make many sounds. They send these sounds out through their blowholes. The beluga whales at the Shedd Aquarium are good at copying what they hear. They can make noises that sound just like the breathing sounds that scuba divers make!

Speaking of divers, did you ever wonder . . .

11

Who takes care of the aquarium?

Fish must be fed and tanks must be cleaned. Some jobs even have to be done on the other side of the glass!

It takes many people to keep an aquarium going. The people who work directly with the animals are called **aquarists.** They are usually responsible for feeding the animals. Most aquarists know how to scuba dive. They often put on wet suits and dive into a tank to feed fish by hand.

Feeding fish in the Kelp Forest at California's Monterey Bay Aquarium

Many people volunteer at aquariums. This means that they work for free. Volunteers can prepare food for the animals. They also might help visitors find their way around.

One of the most important jobs at the aquarium is done by the **veterinarian,** or animal doctor. It's not an easy job. Patients at the aquarium can't tell the doctor where they hurt or how they feel. The veterinarian has to observe the animal. If it's not eating or is behaving strangely, it may need help.

A scientist holds a Moses smoothhound shark at the Marine Lab at the University of Haifa, Israel.

Speaking of strange behavior, did you ever wonder . . .

13

Why do some fish swim in schools?

It looks like there are a million of them! The fish swim very close to one another. Then they all seem to turn on cue.

Fish swim in **schools,** or groups, for several reasons. The main reason is for protection. A school of fish can confuse an enemy. It's hard to pick out just one fish when so many swim together. When they are attacked, most of the fish in the school can get away.

Schooling also makes it easier for the fish to find food. Many eyes looking for a meal are better than just a few. When one fish finds food, the rest can follow.

14

A school of black bar soldier fish

How do all the fish stay together? They use their senses. A fish learns to keep just the right distance from other fish by using its senses of sight, hearing, and sometimes even smell.

Fish also use a special structure called a **lateral line** to help them stay together. The lateral line runs along the side of a fish's body. Special cells in the lateral line help a fish sense the movement of other fish around it.

Speaking of special structures, did you ever wonder . . .

Why are the animals all so different?

Sea star

They both live in the ocean, but an octopus and a shark are very different creatures.

Animals in the ocean are as different in looks and behavior as animals on land. All animals have special characteristics, called **adaptations.** Adaptations help animals survive in their habitats.

Sharks, for example, have adaptations that make them good hunters. A shark's body has a special shape. That shape lets it move through the water using as little energy as possible. Sharks also have a very good sense of smell. Some sharks can pick up odors that are more than 90 meters (about 98 yards) away. That's almost the length of a football field.

An octopus is shy and likes to hide in rocks. It can flatten its body and squeeze through even the smallest cracks in the rocks. It can also change colors and blend into its surroundings to hide. If attacked, an octopus can shoot out a stream of ink. That distracts its enemy long enough for the octopus to get away.

Speaking of survival, did you ever wonder . . .

Silvertip shark

How do aquariums take care of their babies?

Pelagic sting ray

From seahorses to sea otters—there are many different kinds of babies. How do aquariums take care of the newborns?

Most baby fish don't need special care. When they are very small, they are sometimes taken to a separate tank—so that the other fish won't eat them.

Some aquariums, however, take on special nursery jobs. For example, the Monterey Bay Aquarium in California rescues baby sea otters. And these little ocean animals need lots of attention.

18

Sometimes baby sea otters get separated from their mothers. Then they can be in real trouble. People from the Monterey Bay Aquarium raise these pups.

Baby sea otters need constant care. At first they are fed from a bottle. As they grow older, they must learn to catch sea stars and crabs. Divers from the aquarium actually take the otters out into the bay and teach them how to dive. If the otters learn enough, they can return to their natural habitat to live.

Baby otter at Monterey Bay Aquarium

Speaking of natural habitats, did you ever wonder . . .

How do aquariums protect the underwater animals they keep?

Conserve and protect is the message of the day.

Most of Earth is covered with water. Yet many of us know very little about the world beneath our oceans, lakes, and rivers. Aquariums help people learn about the underwater world. When we know more about these important habitats, we can all take steps to protect them.

Aquariums also help underwater animals that are in danger of becoming extinct. Sometimes aquariums shelter animals until they can be returned to their natural habitat. Aquariums also raise babies to release into the wild. This gives the wild population a better chance to survive.

Aquariums are full of interesting things to see. What you learn today at an aquarium can help you make better decisions tomorrow to protect the underwater world.

Touch pool at
Monterey Bay Aquarium

Speaking of the future, did you ever wonder . . .

Manatees, such as this calf, are often harmed by motorboats that travel through the waters where they live.

How can I find out more?

Read On!

Many wonderful books have been written about underwater creatures. From coral reefs to freshwater lakes, there are lots of underwater habitats and lots of interesting stories to read.

Earle, Sylvia, and Wolcott Henry. *Hello Fish! Visiting the Coral Reef.* National Geographic, 2001.

Kalman, Bobbie, and Allison Larin. *What Is a Fish?* Crabtree Publishing, 1998.

Taylor, Barbara, and Jane Burton. *Look Closer: Coral Reef.* DK Pub Merchandise, 2000.

Log On!

Many aquariums have interesting websites. You can learn about their animals at the following sites:

Visit the Monterey Bay's "E-Quarium" at
http://www.montereybayaquarium.org

Visit the Shedd Aquarium in Chicago at
http://www.sheddnet.org

Sea turtle swimming near coral, Great Barrier Reef, Australia

Imagine That!

Sea turtles hatch from eggs that female turtles bury on sandy beaches. But they spend most of their lives swimming around the oceans. Imagine you can travel with a sea turtle. Write a story telling about the wonderful things you would see in the sea.

Baby sea turtles

Glossary

adaptation—a structure or behavior that helps an animal survive

aquarist—a person who takes care of the sea creatures at an aquarium

habitat—a place where a plant or animal lives

invertebrates—animals without backbones

lateral line—a special structure along the body of a fish that helps it sense movement

mammals—groups of warm-blooded animals that breathe air, have backbones, and nurse their young

schools—groups of fish swimming together for protection

tentacles—long, arm-like structures of jellyfish and other invertebrates

veterinarian—a doctor who takes care of animals